the flap pamphlet series

She Can Still Sing

open, read, turn

She Can Still Sing

the flap pamphlet series (No. 23)
Printed and Bound in the United Kingdom

Published by the flap series, 2021
the pamphlet series of flipped eye publishing
All Rights Reserved

Cover Design by Petraski
Series Design © flipped eye publishing, 2010

Author Photo © Robert Golden
First Edition
Copyright © Louisa Adjoa Parker 2021

ISBN-13: 978-1-905233-68-7

She Can Still Sing

Louisa Adjoa Parker

For Leonie
in loving memory
of your beautiful mum, Tasha

Contents | *She Can Still Sing*

Birds

I

Are you the blackbird
with a custard-yellow beak
and blue-black feathers
the exact shade of your hair,
who hops down
from a bramble hedge
lands at my feet,
as though to greet me?

II

In the square in Zurich
while trams move all around us
a sparrow lies face-down
on the frozen ground, wet wings
spread wide, as though
she fell from the sky like rain,
and liked the cold earth so much
she wanted to become part of it.

III

Are you one of the starlings
taking flight in formation,
a blur of black wings
moving through the winter sky?

IV

To mend a small bird's wing,
catch her, cup her in your hands.
Do not squeeze her wings.
Strap the broken wing
tight to her. Place her
in a birdcage. Feed her water.
Feed her seeds. When she's better,
let her fly.

You loved that boy

from the moment
you set eyes on him,
thumb out, standing
at the roadside. Of course
we stopped and let him in.
To us he was the Hat Man –
dark hair curling around his neck,
lashes long as a calf's, an array
of coloured hats. He mixed records
on his decks, made tapes
for his friends. You even
looked alike – tall, long-limbed,
dark-haired. Once you bought –
and somehow rocked
– matching, rainbow jumpers.

Dancer

We'd part our hair in two –
yours thick black waves, mine curly
frizz – and wear it in two buns

atop our heads like Minnie Mouse's ears.
We'd stick red Bindis
on our foreheads; they seemed at home,

fine paste jewels on our brown skins.
We wore platforms on our feet;
I coveted your buffaloes.

We'd dance in half-dark spaces,
move to the sound of bass
your boyfriend spinning records

on black decks, our cheeks sparkling
as flecks of glitter
caught the light.

Light

The world is washed in light –
the kind that comes
after it's been raining –
spread over honeyed stone,
slate roof tiles, the pale cheeks
of a baby blowing raspberries
in the post office. I stare skyward,
as though I'll find you
tucked behind grey clouds
in a patch of gold.

The way you said your name

As though it was a stretchy sweet
you rolled around your mouth
As though it was a gift wrapped
in tissue, tied with curling ribbon.
As though it was soft rain
or sea-spray on your tongue.
As though it was music, rising and falling.
As though it was birdsong.
As though you'd mixed accents
like a cocktail, sweet and sharp
and dark and long.
As though you'd discovered
the sound of your voice
for the first time.
As though each time you said it
you were a tiny girl, reborn.

roots

somewhere along the line
we decided – without words –
we were family. although

the combination of your dad/our mum

didn't last for long, our families
stayed linked,
two tall trees entwined at the roots

Jembe

We'd take our jembes to the beach
sit on sand, bang out rhythms

the hollow slap of skin on skin
bouncing off the rocks.

We'd teach our children how to play;
once, you took my daughter busking.

How I'd longed for one: the wood,
hard, blue rope, bits of goat fur

still attached. You bought it for me.
And when we drummed together,

people gathered round us,
as though we were a fire.

There are moments I forget

like the dark canopy of trees
lining the road from Uplyme,
the grey pebbles on the beach,
the hills we climbed
pushing our babies in buggies,

the silver light over Lyme Bay,
the plump white moon that looked
as though it would fall into the sea;
the wine-red carpet, musty velvet
curtains in the drawing room at Rosehill;

the grapes rotting on the vine outside.

You are at the root of me. It's hard
to say *this happened on that day*,
or *that happened the next*, because
you are part of everything, there
or not there; it seems as though

we only spoke last week.
Your voice, there,
as it has always been,
saying my name
like a song.

Laugh

The day we realised you
had given your laugh to your daughter,

we sat on the brown, zebra-print sofa,
and laughed. The sound of you

two laughing the same laugh
was the funniest thing we'd ever heard.

And we laughed, you, me and our girls,
till our cheeks ached; it was an orchestra,

a sound bath of joy, notes of our ringing
laughter suspended from the beam like music.

bird

a bird
     with broken wings
          still has a voice
               she can still sing

A Butterfly in February

This morning I found a peacock butterfly
trapped in my room, beating crimson wings
against the glass of a window which can never
be opened.   I was scared if I brushed dust
from your wings you might die, so
I scooped your patterned form onto white paper;
you rested your black legs for a moment, folded
your wings shut as if in prayer.

pure

and she's new as a tree-bud, unfurling
and clear as a high note in a hymn
and she's never felt more holy
and she's a bird with mended wings
and the volume is turned down now
and she's glittering like stardust
and He is all around her
and there is
                    no fear
                        just peace
and she is
          new love
                  new light

Everyday Things I Find You In

The yellow morning light that spills
around the edges of my curtains
The sky at night, with silver moon
The sky when it's about to rain
The sun breaking through the clouds
The line of silhouetted trees on the hilltop
The low white mist spilling over fields
The snowdrops in my garden, pushing
up through the earth – heads bent

Bloom

Like the tulips Poppy brought me
when she heard, we all bloom and touch
the lives of those around us, before
it's time to fade.

You were bright as the magenta purples
and butter-yellows of the tulips
on my table, in a fuchsia-pink glass vase,

the ray of light showing up
the veins in their thin petals.

You're

You're in the blues and carmine-reds
and golds of the paint you brushed
onto canvases, in the word *Love*
written in the corner of a canvas
washed in pink.
You're in the sunlight pooling
on the floor, elongating shadows
of the mourner's legs.
You're suspended
in the glittering dust, in the notes
of our voices as we sing.
You're in your daughter's laugh,
at the edges of her smile. In your brother's lips,
your nephew's black hair, in the petals
of the white orchids fallen on the table.

Your brother and his son

Your brother is striding towards us
on long legs, pushing his boy
in a buggy. Perhaps grief's
made me crazy – or perhaps
because you were like my sister – for a moment
it's as though he's *my* long-lost brother, returning.

His little boy is bright as a new day.
He likes an audience, shuffles his feet
like a penguin. He's too young
to know. When I say goodbye,
I hold him close, press kisses
into his sweet, dark hair.

I'll find you

I'll find you strumming your guitar
and singing, cross-legged on the ground,

or walking in the mountains, breathing
in the clean Swiss air.

I'll find you picnicking by the lake
in Zurich or cooking at the rehab.

I'll find you making friends with strangers
or sipping Teh tarik in Malaysia.

I'll find you climbing out of your aunt's window
running across the neighbours' lawns.

I'll find you on the road to Charmouth
pushing your baby up the hill.

I'll find you moving between airports,
rucksack on your back.

I'll find you playing in the garden
at Rosehill or tidying the house.

I'll find you with a paintbrush
dipped in starlight.

Wings

Wings sprout
from her shoulder blades
like buds of new, clean leaves.
She soars into a dark sky,
flies over trams, rooftops,
white mountain peaks.
Night air rushes over her
as she rises, kissing feathers,
kissing skin. Her wingtips
brush the moon, the stars.
She glides, then dips, and soars.

Time

Snowdrops dissolve back into the earth,
winds blow around our garden.

I drive past a haze of bluebells,
purpling the roadside.
I plant sage and rosemary

and thyme, remember meals
we shared. Some days, sun warms
my cold skin. Still, I talk to you

out loud. Still, I press my fingers
to my lips,
touch them to your face,

which will no longer be changed
by time now, but will remain
smiling behind glass.

Housewarming

August. Nights are drawing in.
Two decades on, your daughter
has returned to the patch of land
she came from. We're in her garden:
long stretch of lawn, next door's
one-eyed dog ambling over grass.
Flower lights hang from the washing line.
Your hammock strung on wooden posts.
In the distance, yellow fields, a vast,
pale sky. Her grandmother's farm.
Wasps hover too close to us, giddy
with the scent of beer. A burning log
sends sprays of orange into night air.
Bats fly overhead. Howard plays
dancehall, funk, head bent, his decks
swapped for a laptop. His beard
is white, the children grown now,
but it's as though time
has stood still and I'll turn and see you
next to me. Instead, I'm dancing
with our grown-up daughters
under a scattering of stars.

Acknowledgments

Acknowledgements are due to the editors of Irisi and Acumen, publications in which some of the poems first appeared.

Big thanks go to Arts Council England for supporting the mentoring of this collection; Pascale Petit for said mentoring; Leonie Prater for giving this collection her blessing; family, friends and colleagues who have supported my work, including Christina Palfrey; Peter Fry; my daughters Keziah Bell, Jessie Parker and Alicia Parker; Lottie Prowse, Melissa Merrington-Pink, Caitlin Miller, Maisie Hill, Clare Johnson, Jemima Moore, Poppy Kennedy, and Louise-Boston-Mammah; my grandchildren Maya, Leila, Harrison and Billy (most of whom are too little to read yet but thank you for coming into my life); and finally, biggest thanks of all to Natasha Rajaratnam, for enriching mine, my family's, and so many other people's lives with your light and friendship.